Private Practice, On Purpose

A Physician's Guide to Launching a Practice That Works

Brittney T. Anderson, MD

Golden Ivy Co

Contents

Author's Note

This book was written for physicians who are thinking, often quietly, about private practice. Not because they are reckless or dissatisfied with medicine itself. But because something about the way they are practicing no longer fits.

If you're looking for a quick-start manual, a guaranteed formula, or a promise that everything will be easy, this book is not for you. Private practice is work. It requires planning, responsibility, and thoughtful decision-making.

This book is for physicians who want clarity, not hype.

Not long after opening my own practice, I told myself that if the practice was stable and successful after a few years, I would write a book to help other physicians navigate this process with more clarity than I had at the beginning. My private practice has been incredibly successful, and this book is the result of that commitment.

You may find that this book raises questions before it answers them; that is intentional and hopefully will help you build clarity. The clarity required to plan a private practice often comes from giving yourself space to think. I believe that building a private practice works best when decisions are made deliberately, not reactively.

There is no single right age, stage, or moment to consider private practice. There is only the moment when you begin asking better questions about how you want your work, and your life, to look.

Whether you ultimately choose private practice or decide that employment fits you better right now, this book has done its job if it helps you decide intentionally. That alone is progress.

Introduction

Why This Book Exists

Most physicians don't wake up one day and suddenly decide to open a private practice.

Instead, the thought often creeps in quietly.

It shows up after another late evening of charting. After another meeting where decisions are made about your work without you in the room. After realizing you are practicing medicine in a system that no longer feels aligned with how you want to care for patients or how you want to live your life.

For many physicians, private practice begins not as a plan, but as a question:

Could I do this differently?

Is ownership even realistic anymore?

Would starting my own practice give me freedom or just a different kind of stress?

I wrote this book because I've been on both sides of those questions.

After training, I worked in two very different employed models and eventually made the decision to step away and build my own private practice. That decision was not impulsive and it wasn't driven by dissatisfaction alone. It was driven by a desire to practice medicine with intention, autonomy, and sustainability.

What I learned along the way, and what too few physicians are taught, is that private practice is not about rebellion or risk-taking for the sake of it. It is about design. The practices that last are not built accidentally or emotionally. They are built thoughtfully, with clarity and purpose.

Private practice is hard. But so is medicine.

The difference is that this kind of hard is one you can design. You can shape the systems, the schedule, the team, and the structure in ways that support both patient care and your life. And when something isn't working, you're allowed to change it.

Unfortunately, most physicians are offered only extremes when it comes to private practice advice. On one end, they are warned that ownership is outdated, impossible, or irresponsible. On the other, they are sold an oversimplified narrative that ignores cash flow, staffing, compliance, burnout, and real life. Neither of these stories is helpful. And neither reflects the reality I see every day working with physicians across the country who have a dream of private practice ownership.

This book exists to fill that gap.

Private Practice, On Purpose is not meant to convince you that private practice is the right answer. It is meant to help you ask better questions. It will help you think through what ownership could look like for you based on your goals, your season of life, and your tolerance for risk and responsibility.

Throughout this book, you will be guided to slow down and think intentionally about your vision, your business model, your finances, your operations, and your capacity. You will be encouraged to put ideas on paper before putting money on the line. And you will be reminded repeatedly that the goal is not just to open a practice, but to build one that actually works.

This book is structured to be practical. It is not filled with theory or trends. Instead, it reflects real decisions physicians must make and the common missteps that derail otherwise strong clinicians. You do not need to have all the answers before you begin reading. You simply need a willingness to be honest about what you want...and what you don't.

A Note on How This Book Is Organized

If you've practiced medicine for any length of time, you already know how to think through complex problems.

You start with the story, what's being experienced and felt by the patient. You look at the facts in front of you. You identify what's actually going on. And then you decide how to move forward. That same rhythm shows up throughout this book.

Many of the chapters follow a familiar flow: the lived experience, the objective reality, an honest assessment, and a practical way to think about next steps. In medical school, we called this the SOAP format. It helped us organize complex information, make sense of uncertainty, and decide what to do next. If that framework was good enough to guide us through patient care, it's good enough to help us think through building a practice. Not because business decisions are the same as clinical ones, but because physicians already know how to reason through uncertainty, weigh tradeoffs, and make thoughtful plans.

You are not being asked to learn how to think in a new way. You're being invited to use skills you already have in a different context. You won't see S-O-A-P labeled on every page and you don't need to memorize anything. It's simply the structure guiding the conversation, a quiet framework underneath the chapters to help keep things clear, grounded, and practical.

If you are reading this book because you feel stuck, curious, restless, or quietly hopeful, you're in the right place. Private practice, when done well, is not accidental. It is intentional. And the work of building it begins long before you sign a lease or open your doors. Let's start there.

Section I: Permission and Perspective

If you're reading this, I imagine it comes at the end of a long stretch of hard days.

Maybe it's late at night, when the house is finally quiet and your mind won't shut off. Or maybe it's the first slow moment you've had in days, early in the morning, on a weekend, or between responsibilities, when you finally let yourself think about the thought you've been pushing down:

There has to be another way to practice medicine.

Clinic ran long again. Something that should have been simple wasn't. You tried to make a small change, one you knew would help, and you were reminded that it wasn't your decision to make.

Maybe you talked it through with your spouse or a colleague. Or maybe you've been carrying the thought quietly on your own: *I can't keep doing this forever.*

And then that familiar voice showed up:

Private practice sounds nice, but it's probably not realistic.

It's too hard now. It's not profitable.

People like me don't do that.

If any of that sounds familiar, you're exactly where many physicians find themselves when they first start thinking about private practice. Not energized and bold, but tired, frustrated, and quietly curious.

This section exists for one reason: permission.

Not permission to quit your job tomorrow. Not permission to blow up your life. But permission to seriously consider whether private practice might actually be possible for you.

Because here's what I've learned both in my own journey and in working with other physicians: Most employed physicians don't avoid private practice because they aren't capable. They avoid it because the stories they've been told about it feel overwhelming, risky, or outdated.

They've been told it's not profitable. That it's too complicated. That if you didn't do it right out of training, you missed your chance. Over time, those messages start to feel like facts. They aren't.

Private practice is work. It does require planning, decision-making, and discomfort. But it is not reserved for a special personality type, a different generation, or someone with a business degree. And it is not inherently less stable or less profitable than employment, despite what you may have been led to believe.

This section isn't about logistics yet, we'll get there. It's about stepping back and examining the assumptions you're carrying, often without even realizing it.

Assumptions like:

I'm not cut out to run a business.

I don't know enough to do this safely.

It's probably easier to just stay where I am.

Many of those beliefs seem to make sense. They're protective. They're often reinforced by training, by employers, and by well-meaning people who worry about you. But they're also incomplete. You already make complex decisions every day. You already manage risk. You already balance competing priorities with limited resources. You are not starting from zero.

By the end of this section, I don't need you to feel ready. I don't even need you to feel confident. If nothing else, I want you to feel this: Private practice is not completely impossible. And maybe, just maybe, the dissatisfaction you're feeling isn't a personal failing or a phase you have to push through. Maybe it's a signal worth paying attention to.

This book is written physician to physician. Not from a pedestal. Not with hype. And not with the assumption that there's one "right" way to start a private practice. My goal isn't to convince you that private practice is the answer for everyone. It isn't. My goal is to help you see the process clearly so you can decide what you want your future in medicine to look like, without fear, exaggeration, or myths getting in the way.

So take a breath. You don't have to decide anything right now.

For now, let's just talk honestly about what you've been told, and what might actually be true.

When Wanting More Stopped Feeling Wrong

Straight out of residency, like most of my peers, I went into employed practice. I started at a federally qualified health center and stayed there for two years. In many ways, it was exactly where I wanted to be, serving an underserved population and caring for patients who truly needed better access to care.

But even when the mission felt right, the day-to-day reality was hard.

Some days I didn't have a nurse. Some days I didn't have a receptionist. And some days, I had neither. It was just me trying to see patients, answer phones, room patients, and provide good care all at once. I did the best I could, but it was unsustainable.

When I left that first position, I moved into academic medicine. On paper, it was a great fit. I could teach medical students and residents while still practicing clinically. But if you've ever worked in academic medicine, you know one of the main frustrations: recognizing that something needs to change, but having to navigate layers of systems and approvals to make even small improvements. There's nothing inherently wrong with that structure, but I quickly realized it wasn't one in which I thrived.

The longer I remained in employed roles, the harder it became to ignore a growing sense that this wasn't how I wanted to practice medicine long-term.

The physicians I had admired growing up, the ones I shadowed in high school and medical school, were almost all in private practice. But somewhere between those early experiences and completing residency, that path had quietly disappeared from the conversation. Private practice wasn't discussed much during training, and when it was, it was often framed as outdated, risky, or no longer viable.

Within five years of completing residency, I had reached burnout.

Before then, burnout was a term I associated with long hours or unfinished charts. In my mind it was something that happened to physicians who were overworked or disorganized. But that wasn't what this felt like. The issue wasn't the number of hours I was working. It was that I was practicing within systems that didn't allow me to thrive.

I hadn't built a professional life that aligned with my strengths or protected my energy. I didn't have autonomy and I didn't have ownership. And over time, that misalignment was exhausting.

After a particularly difficult stretch, I booked a flight to Honolulu. I didn't go to escape my responsibilities, I went because I needed space, away from the daily noise, so I could ask myself some honest questions. Sitting on the beach, I thought about what I wanted my career to look like ten and twenty years down the road. I asked myself what I would need in order to have a long, sustainable, and fulfilling career in medicine. And for the first time, I allowed myself to take the idea of private practice seriously. Not as a reckless leap, but as a thoughtful, intentional option.

That trip didn't give me all the answers. But it did give me clarity. It helped me realize that staying where I was simply because it felt safer wasn't actually safe at all. It was slowly pulling me away from the kind of physician, and person, I wanted to be.

I didn't make a quick decision to leave employed practice. That's not my style. I made lots of pros and cons lists. And every time, the same thing happened: the pros outweighed the cons. It was clear. I wanted more autonomy, I wanted alignment, and I wanted to rediscover my joy in practicing medicine.

Still, wanting private practice didn't make the decision any less scary. I didn't have formal business training, I didn't have an MBA, and I didn't know exactly where to start when it came to building a practice. But I did know that staying where I was wasn't sustainable.

So I made the decision.

When I returned home from Hawaii, I submitted my letter of resignation. And from that moment forward, my focus shifted from whether I *could* do this to *how* I would do it.

I knew the practice wouldn't be perfect. But it would be mine. And because it was mine, it would be something I could work on to make better over time. I wasn't chasing more for the sake of ambition or ego. I was responding to a quiet, persistent feeling that the way I was practicing medicine no longer fit who I was becoming.

Wanting more wasn't the problem. Ignoring it would have been.

CHAPTER 1

Wanting More Doesn't Require Another Degree

When I started planning my practice, I didn't feel ready. I felt unprepared and unqualified, and I initially believed the missing piece was a business degree.

I had never taken a business class. I didn't know the language and I didn't know the rules. But I did know a physician who had opened her own practice after getting an MBA. So somewhere along the way, I absorbed the idea that this was the responsible way to do it. I believed that if a physician was serious about private practice, they needed formal business training first. I assumed that without it, I was behind before I even began.

What intimidated me most wasn't the idea of running a business in general, it was the financial language. The terms. The acronyms. The way conversations seemed to move quickly, as if I should already understand things I'd never been taught.

My CPA was incredibly helpful. But I distinctly remember sitting in meetings with him writing down words he used with question marks next to them, then going home and Googling them later. I wasn't confused because I was incapable. I was confused because this was new.

What bothered me was the expectation, mostly self-imposed, that I should understand everything immediately. That expectation came straight from medical training. In medicine, perfection matters. Precision matters. Lives depend on it. We're trained to believe that not knowing something is dangerous and that mistakes are unacceptable.

But this wasn't life or death. That realization changed everything for me. Once I understood that starting a private practice didn't require perfection, only progression, the pressure lifted. I didn't need to master every concept before moving forward, I could learn as I went. I could ask questions. I could ask people to slow down and explain things again.

I also realized something else that mattered: an MBA would have been far broader than what I actually needed. I didn't need to understand every facet of business in the abstract. I needed to understand *my* business. I needed someone who could help me think through finances, taxes, and structure in a practical way. And that's exactly what my CPA was there for.

What I really needed wasn't a business degree. I needed confidence in myself. The confidence that I could learn what I needed to know and that I could use the resources around me to fill in the gaps.

Private practice doesn't require you to become a different person. It doesn't require you to go back to school or earn another set of credentials before you're "allowed" to begin. It requires you to be willing to start without knowing everything.

If you're stuck here, feeling like you need more training, more credentials, or more preparation before you can even take the first step, I want you to know this: You don't need a business degree. You just need to get started. Everything else can be learned along the way.

CHAPTER 2

Rethinking Profitability in Private Practice

When employed physicians talk about private practice and money, the concern is usually the same: the financial risk feels too high.

You may worry that no bank will loan you the money you need. You may assume it will take a long time before you're able to pay yourself. You may picture months, or longer, without income. And for physicians with families or other responsibilities, that fear can feel paralyzing.

Underneath all of it is a deeper concern: instability.

Compared to the steady paycheck you're used to as an employee, private practice can feel unpredictable and unsafe. And when you're already exhausted from your current job, it's easy to decide that even an imperfect guarantee is better than an unknown.

But that comparison deserves a closer look.

As an employed physician, your paycheck feels guaranteed because it arrives on time and without much thought. What you don't see is the full financial picture behind it. You're not given access to how revenue is generated, how expenses are managed, or how decisions are made that directly affect what you earn.

In private practice, that picture becomes visible. Most physicians misunderstand profitability because they confuse predictability with security.

Employment feels safer because it's familiar, not because it's immune to change. Salaries get cut. Contracts change. Schedules shift. Productivity expectations increase. The sense of security we have in employment often comes from not seeing the math. Ownership changes that.

The real shift happens when you sit down and actually do the math.

Instead of asking, *Will this be profitable?* you start asking different questions:

What do I need to bring home?

What does that mean my practice needs to generate?

What expenses are required to support that?

What decisions do I control?

For many physicians, this is the first time they've ever been asked to think about income this way. Not as a fixed number handed to them, but as something that can be designed, measured, and adjusted.

Profitability in private practice isn't accidental. It isn't reserved for a certain specialty or practice model. It's the result of understanding revenue, being intentional about expenses, and making decisions with clarity instead of fear.

If you're worried about money, it's worth knowing that there are physicians in your same specialty who are making more in private practice than they ever did as employed physicians. Not because they are over-charging or being fraudulent. Not because they are working twice as many hours. But because they were willing to look at the numbers instead of avoiding them.

CHAPTER 3

Perfectionism as a Barrier to Starting

Medical training teaches you that mistakes matter.

Details matter. Precision matters. In many situations, lives depend on it. Over time, that lesson becomes internalized, not just as professional responsibility, but as identity. You learn to prepare exhaustively, to anticipate every possible outcome, and to avoid moving forward until you're confident you've accounted for everything.

That mindset serves you well in patient care. But when it comes to starting a private practice, it can work against you.

For me, perfectionism showed up most clearly in workflow. I wanted every process mapped out exactly. I obsessed over how patients would move through the clinic, how staff would handle each step, and how everything would function together on day one. Instead of creating a solid plan and trusting that it would evolve, I kept revisiting it. I was convinced that if I just thought about it a little longer, I could make it flawless.

The same thing happened with the physical space. I stressed myself out wanting every room set up perfectly before we opened. Every piece of furniture in place. Every supply accounted for. Looking back, we had more than enough to get started, and my insistence on perfection only added unnecessary stress.

That urge for perfection didn't come from ego; it came from training. In medicine, being unprepared can have serious consequences. In business, especially early on, being unfinished is often part of the process.

No practice opens fully optimized. No workflow survives the first contact with real patients exactly as designed. Early days are not a final exam, they're information-gathering.

I realized this about halfway through our first day.

Things weren't perfect, but they were working. The flow started to make sense. Adjustments happened in real time. What felt overwhelming in theory became manageable in practice. And the clarity I had been chasing before opening came not from more planning, but from actually doing the work.

That's the shift most perfectionist physicians need to make. The practice itself is not life or death, the care you provide is. Your energy deserves to be focused on excellence in patient care, not on achieving a fictional version of perfection in systems that are meant to evolve. When perfectionism shows up in this process, it often sounds responsible. It tells you you're just being careful and thorough. But more often than not, it's fear in professional clothing.

The goal at the beginning isn't perfection. The goal is safe, compliant, functional, and adaptable. Ready doesn't mean finished. Ready means you've built something solid enough to learn from.

If you're waiting for the moment when everything feels perfectly in place, that moment may never come. Not because you're incapable, but because private practice isn't static. It grows, it adjusts, and it improves with time.

CHAPTER 4

Becoming a CEO

Before private practice, the word CEO didn't feel like it belonged anywhere near my name.

It often brings to mind someone sitting in an office all day, attending meetings, speaking in business jargon, and being far removed from patient care. Even though many physicians successfully run their own practices, it can be hard to picture how that identity fits with being a clinician.

Becoming a CEO doesn't mean stepping away from patient care. It means adding a new lens. You begin to think not only about the patient in front of you, but about the structure that supports their care. You consider the schedule, the workflow, the finances, the people, and the long-term sustainability of the practice.

For many physicians, the shift happens when ownership becomes concrete, when responsibility can't be deferred or delegated away. When the decisions are no longer hypothetical, that's when the role changes.

The uncomfortable part of the shift to CEO is often the weight of responsibility. Ownership expands what you're accountable for. It's no longer just your work, it's the livelihoods of the people you employ and the systems that allow the practice to function.

For many physicians, the CEO role feels abstract at first. It's hard to know what it actually looks like in real life, especially early on when you're still very much in patient care. One practical way to begin stepping into this role is to protect intentional "CEO time" each week. This doesn't have to be a full day. For some physicians, it starts as a few hours a week or a half day. This is time that is not for charting or catching up on messages. It's time for thinking like an owner: reviewing finances, looking at schedules, identifying bottlenecks, planning ahead, or asking, *What does this practice need from me right now?* Early on, this kind of time creates clarity. Over time, it creates confidence. It's often during these quiet, intentional moments that physicians begin to feel the shift into ownership.

What surprises many physicians is how natural this role becomes over time. With organization and intentional mindset work, the balance between clinician and owner starts to feel less like a performance and more like alignment. Decision-making becomes clearer. Leadership becomes part of how you practice, not something separate from it.

Being a CEO doesn't mean being stuffy or business-obsessed. It means being able to hold both: excellent patient care and a well-run practice. You don't need to feel confident before you begin. You don't need to have everything figured out. You just need to be willing to step into the role and grow into it over time.

CHAPTER 5

Dealing With Doubt

When you start thinking seriously about private practice, doubt almost always shows up.

Not necessarily as a loud objection, but as a steady undercurrent of questions, hesitations, and warnings that make you pause. Often, that doubt doesn't come from a single place, it comes from patterns you've been immersed in for years.

For many physicians, doubt related to private practice starts in training. In some training environments, private practice is barely mentioned at all. Or it's framed as outdated, unrealistic, or unnecessarily difficult. When you don't see something done, it's easy to assume it isn't viable. And for that reason, most graduates move directly into employed practice after their training.

Doubt can also come from the people who care about you most. Spouses, close friends, and family members may raise concerns about time, income, and stability. These questions are usually rooted in protection, not discouragement. They reflect understandable fears about risk, especially when the path forward isn't clearly defined yet.

And then there's doubt within medicine itself. Even among physicians, there's still a lot of uncertainty surrounding private practice. You may hear statements like:

Private practice is dead.

It's too risky now.

You'll lose money.

You can't take care of patients and run a business.

These statements tend to sound authoritative, especially when they're repeated often. But repetition doesn't make them universally true. What matters is learning how to respond to doubt; not by ignoring it, but by discerning it.

The truth is, some doubts are actually worth listening to. Questions about money, sustainability, and feasibility should slow you down, but they should not stop you. They're signals to run the numbers, think carefully, and make sure the math works. When used well, these questions make your plan stronger. They push you toward clarity instead of assumptions.

Other doubts are less useful. Statements that question your ability, your intelligence, or your capacity to learn don't lead to better decisions. They don't sharpen your thinking, they undermine it. Those kinds of doubts aren't warnings, they're noise.

Part of moving forward thoughtfully is learning the difference. Doubt doesn't mean you're on the wrong path. It means you need to pause, get clarity, and decide intentionally. When you stop treating doubt as a stop sign and start treating it as a prompt, it loses much of its power. Doubt is not a verdict, it's information.

Section I was not about certainty. It was about perspective.

You examined some of the most common concerns physicians have about private practice: that you need more credentials, that it's financially irresponsible, that everything must be perfect before you begin, or that doubt means you shouldn't move forward. None of those beliefs make you weak or naïve. They make sense in the context of medical training and employment.

But they are not the whole story.

With a clearer perspective, you're now in a position to move forward thoughtfully and with intention.

Section II: Designing the Practice You're Building

By the time you reach this section, something important has shifted. You're no longer asking whether private practice is possible. You're starting to imagine what your practice could look like. This is where many physicians get into trouble. Not because they lack motivation or intelligence, but because they underestimate how much freedom they actually have.

After years of training and employment, it's easy to assume there's a "right" way to build a practice. You may find yourself defaulting to what you've seen before: the model you trained in, the system you work in now, or the structure of another practice that seems successful from the outside.

But private practice doesn't require replication.

One of the biggest mistakes physicians make at this stage is leaving employment in search of more freedom, only to build a practice that ties them down just as tightly, sometimes more so. Longer hours. Less flexibility. Decisions driven by habit instead of thoughtfulness. This usually isn't intentional. It happens when clarity comes too late.

Section II exists to slow you down. Not to stall momentum, but to direct it.

Before you choose a location, hire staff, or invest in systems, you need to be clear about the kind of practice you're building and the kind of life it's meant to support. These early decisions ripple outward. They shape your schedule, your finances, your stress level, and your sustainability far more than most physicians realize at the outset.

This is the stage where jumping ahead feels productive and where it's most costly.

So instead of asking, *What do most practices do?* ask *What actually works for me?*

The chapters in this section will help you think intentionally about how you want to practice, who you want to serve, how your time will be structured, and what kind of flexibility you're truly building toward. There's no single correct answer here. But there is a cost to building without clarity.

By the end of this section, you should be able to describe your practice. Not in vague terms, but in choices that feel aligned, realistic, and sustainable. Not perfect, not final, but intentionally yours.

From here, everything else becomes easier to decide.

Building What You Meant to Leave

I often meet physicians at a certain point.

They've decided to leave employment. They feel lighter already, relieved, even. The idea of private practice feels energizing, full of possibility. For the first time in a long time, they're imagining something different.

And then they start planning.

At first, the decisions seem straightforward. They sketch out a schedule that looks a lot like the one they're used to. They assume they'll offer the same services they've always provided. They think about office space based on what they've seen before. None of these choices feel wrong, they feel familiar.

That familiarity is comforting.

What they don't realize yet is that they're quietly rebuilding the very structure they wanted to leave. The hours get longer than intended. Administrative work creeps into evenings. The practice begins to feel busy before it feels intentional. When something doesn't feel quite right, they tell themselves this is just the startup phase and that things will settle down later. But "later" seems like a moving target.

When we slow down and talk through the details, a pattern usually emerges. The practice wasn't designed, it was assembled. Decisions were made quickly, based on what seemed normal or safe, rather than on what actually fit. And it's rarely because the physician didn't care. It's because no one ever told them how much freedom they actually had. They assumed there was a right way to build a practice. A standard model. A default structure. They believed that deviating too much from what they'd seen before was risky when, in reality, copying it without reflection was just as risky.

This is often the moment when things begin to shift. They start asking different questions. Not *What do most practices do?* but *What do I want my days to look like?* Not *What feels expected?* but *What feels sustainable?*

And with that shift, the planning changes. The schedule becomes intentional instead of packed. Services become focused instead of broad. Decisions start to connect to one another rather than pulling in different directions. The practice begins to feel like something they're building rather than something that's happening to them.

The difference isn't motivation or intelligence. It's clarity. And when clarity comes early, private practice stops feeling like a gamble and starts feeling like a design.

CHAPTER 6

Clarifying the Mission

Before you decide on a practice type, a location, or a schedule, there's one thing that needs to come first. The mission.

For many physicians, the idea of a mission statement feels uncomfortable. It sounds corporate, abstract, or disconnected from the real work of taking care of patients. It's often grouped with branding exercises that feel performative rather than practical. That's not how I want you to think about it. Your mission statement is not fluff. It's a foundation.

When physicians skip this step, it shows up quickly. Decisions feel scattered. The practice lacks cohesion. It becomes harder to say no. Every opportunity sounds good because there's no clear reason to turn things down.

Without a mission statement, you don't have a compass.

You may find yourself making decisions based on convenience, fear, or what you've seen other practices do, rather than building something intentionally. Over time, that leads to a practice that feels misaligned. One that technically works, but doesn't quite feel like what you hoped for.

A clear mission statement changes that. Your mission statement anchors what you're building. It's something you can come back to again and again when decisions feel heavy or unclear. It gives structure to your planning and coherence to the practice as it takes shape.

I teach mission statements in a very specific way, because vague language isn't helpful when you're trying to make real decisions.

Here's the format: "Our mission is to [solve the core problem your patients face] for [your ideal patient population] by [your unique approach or values], ultimately leading to [the improved life or transformation you provide] and contributing to [your broader impact]. We envision a practice where [what it looks like, feels like, and sounds like]."

This isn't meant to be poetic. It's meant to be usable.

A good mission statement helps you answer questions like:

Does this service belong here?

Is this schedule aligned with what I'm trying to build?

Does this opportunity move the practice toward or away from its purpose?

Is this growth or just more work?

When your mission statement is clear, decisions get easier. Not easy, but clearer. Without it, every choice feels equally important, and that's exhausting. Your mission statement isn't meant to impress anyone, it's meant to guide you. It should reflect who you want to serve, how you want to practice, what you value, and the kind of impact you want your work to have.

Your mission statement is also allowed to evolve. But starting without one leaves you reacting instead of building. A clear mission statement doesn't answer every question for you, but it gives you something solid to return to when decisions feel heavy or unclear. When your mission is defined, choices stop feeling scattered. Your practice begins to take shape with more coherence and less second-guessing. From here, you're no longer building in pieces. You're building with direction.

CHAPTER 7

Choosing a Practice Model That Fits

Most physicians think choosing a practice model is primarily about money.

Insurance-based. Direct Care. Concierge. Telemedicine. The conversation often starts, and sometimes ends, with revenue assumptions, reimbursement concerns, or what seems most financially "safe."

But in reality, this decision is much less about money than most people think. It's about how you want to practice medicine and how you want your life to look while doing it.

Choosing a practice model is really a decision about flexibility, control, and the way you want to deliver care. It shapes your schedule, your availability, your relationship with patients, and the pace of your days. Money matters, of course, but it's not the best place to start.

When physicians struggle with this decision, it's often because they're reacting instead of designing. One of the biggest mistakes I see is choosing a model based on frustration with previous employment. If you were previously employed in an insurance-based practice and it felt overwhelming, the instinct may be to avoid insurance entirely. If a particular model felt rigid in employment, the temptation may be to swing to the opposite extreme.

But private practice gives you more freedom than that. Just because a model didn't work for you in the past doesn't mean it can't work at all. Often, it just means it wasn't designed intentionally. Or it wasn't designed *for you*.

Another common mistake is not fully understanding what each model actually requires day to day. Every practice type comes with tradeoffs. None of them are "easy," they're just different.

In an insurance-based practice, what physicians don't always realize is that success requires volume and patience. You have to see a certain number of patients, and you have to regularly deal with insurance companies and contracts.

In concierge or membership-based practices, what's often underestimated is the need for consistent marketing. Patients have to be willing to pay out of pocket for your services, which means you must clearly communicate your value. These models also tend to require greater availability and responsiveness.

Telemedicine practices come with their own realities. To scale successfully, many require licensure in multiple states. Insurance coverage can be inconsistent, making it important to have a clear and sustainable pay structure. Strong marketing is essential in a telemedicine practice.

None of these realities are meant to scare you away. They're meant to clarify the decision.

I encourage physicians to choose a practice model by considering:

How they want their day-to-day life to look

What level of income they need and want

How much energy they can devote to marketing

What model supports a happy life with less burnout

This decision doesn't have to be permanent. Practices evolve and models can change. But clarity here matters. The goal isn't to choose the "best" model. It's to choose the one that fits you and commit to it intentionally.

CHAPTER 8

Designing Services That Fit

When physicians design their services, they most commonly start too broad. It feels safer to offer more. You don't want to turn patients away. You don't want to miss opportunities. And in the early stages of building a practice, it can feel reassuring to keep everything on the table. But starting broad is often the fastest way to build a practice that feels overwhelming and unsustainable.

Private practice gives you permission to focus.

You are not required to recreate the full scope of medicine you were trained in. You get to decide which parts of medicine you actually want to practice and which parts you don't.

Your services should be anchored to your mission. They don't need to be copied from another practice. When services are chosen without clarity, the practice feels scattered. But when they're chosen intentionally, the practice feels cohesive.

One of the biggest contributors to burnout is misalignment between services and energy. That misalignment doesn't always show up as exhaustion right away. Sometimes it looks like dreading certain visits, feeling irritable by the end of the day, or noticing that the parts of medicine you once enjoyed now feel heavy. Sometimes it shows up as decision fatigue. When you have too many services pulling your attention in different directions, none of them get your best energy.

When services are chosen without intention, the workday becomes fragmented. Your energy is spent reacting instead of practicing. Over time, even meaningful work can start to feel unsustainable. Not because you're doing too much medicine, but because you're likely doing the wrong mix of it.

This is why starting focused matters. Starting with a focused set of services allows you to build systems, communicate clearly with patients, and protect your time and energy.

This is your practice. Consider the services you actually want to provide, keeping in mind that you can always expand later. You are allowed to say no, you are allowed to refer patients out, and you are allowed to not offer services you don't want to do. Private practice is not about doing everything. It's about doing the right things well. The goal here isn't to narrow your scope out of fear or limitation. It's to help you think more intentionally about the services you offer and how those choices shape your energy, your days, and the sustainability of your practice.

CHAPTER 9

Creating Your Clinic Schedule

Designing your clinic schedule is one of the most consequential decisions you'll make early in private practice. And it is one of the most underestimated.

Your schedule is not just a logistical detail. It's an expression of leadership. Long before you hire staff, finalize services, or grow your patient panel, the way you structure your days communicates what you value to your patients, your team, and yourself.

Once a schedule is set, it tends to become sticky. Patients plan around it. Staff build their lives around it. Expectations form quickly. While schedules can absolutely change over time, adjusting them later often requires more disruption than physicians anticipate. That's why this early decision deserves more attention than it usually gets.

Many physicians default to familiar schedules of five days a week and standard business hours. Not because they've chosen them intentionally, but because they're what we've always known. Training environments and employed positions rarely invite physicians to question whether those structures actually fit their energy, priorities, or lives. Over time, those defaults can create quiet strain. Long clinic days that leave little room for recovery. Schedules that clash with family responsibilities or personal rhythms. Clinic hours that don't actually align with patient demand, but persist simply because they're traditional.

A schedule chosen without intention can slowly undermine even a well-designed practice. Your clinic schedule should be designed in conversation with the work you've already done. It should reflect your mission. It should support your chosen practice model. It should align with the services you plan to offer and the energy those services require.

Designing your schedule isn't about optimization or productivity. It's about sustainability.

Clinic hours determine how your days feel. They shape your mornings and evenings, your weekdays and weekends. They influence how much margin you have for administrative work, for leadership responsibilities, and for life outside of medicine.

Still, it's important to remember that your first schedule is not a lifelong commitment. You are allowed to learn. You are allowed to notice what works and what doesn't. You are allowed to adjust as your practice grows and your needs change.

Your initial schedule doesn't need to be perfect, but it does need to be thoughtful. The goal is not to predict every future need or contingency. The goal is to start with a structure that reflects your values, supports your energy, and gives your practice room to grow, without costing you the life you're trying to build alongside it.

CHAPTER 10

Understanding Your Brand and Branding

When physicians think about building a brand, many picture logos, color palettes, websites, and fonts. That's understandable. Those elements are visible. They feel concrete. And when you're building something new, it's tempting to start with the pieces that make it look real.

But that's branding. Your brand is something else entirely.

Your brand is how your practice is experienced. It's how patients feel when they walk through the door. It's what they tell friends and family after a visit. It's how staff describe their workday. It's what other clinicians expect when they refer someone to you. In other words, your brand is the story people carry with them after they interact with your practice.

That story is being shaped long before you choose a logo. Your brand begins to take form through the decisions you've already been making in this section: your mission, your practice model, the services you offer, and the way you structure your time. Those choices determine how your practice feels to be in, not just how it looks from the outside.

A practice built around clarity and intention feels different than one built on defaults. Patients notice that difference. Staff feel it. Even if no one ever names it explicitly, the experience leaves an impression. That impression is your brand.

This is why branding, in the traditional sense, is not the starting point. Branding refers to the visual and verbal tools used to communicate your practice to the outside world. Things like logos, color palettes, fonts, websites, and written messaging.

Don't get me wrong, these elements matter. And over time, they help create recognition, consistency, and familiarity. But branding works best when it reflects decisions that have already been made. When your mission is clear, your practice model is defined, your services are aligned with your energy, and your schedule supports the way you want to work, branding becomes an extension of that clarity. When those pieces are aligned, your brand starts to take shape naturally. Branding then becomes a tool, not a task.

Understanding the distinction between your brand and branding keeps your focus where it belongs. Instead of spending energy on appearances too early, you can invest your attention in building a practice that feels coherent, sustainable, and intentional from the inside out.

With that foundation in place, you're ready to think more clearly about how your practice shows up in the world and how the right people come to find it.

Section II was about design. Not design in the visual sense, but in the structural one.

You moved from questioning assumptions to making intentional choices. You clarified what matters to you, how you want to practice, and what kind of structure can support that vision. You considered your mission, your practice model, the services you want to provide, the rhythm of your days, and the experience your practice creates. These should not be isolated decisions but connected ones. None of these choices exist in a vacuum. Together, they form the foundation of a practice that feels coherent rather than reactive.

This section wasn't about finding the "right" answers. It was about recognizing that you have more agency than you may have been taught to expect and that thoughtful design is what allows a practice to be both sustainable and personal.

With this foundation in place, you're no longer imagining a practice in abstract terms. You're beginning to see its shape.

From here, the work shifts. The next section moves from internal design to external reality, turning intention into action and structure into something that can function and grow in the real world.

Section III: Building a Stable Foundation

This is the part of building a private practice that most physicians find the least familiar.

You've spent years learning to make high-stakes clinical decisions, but very little time being taught how businesses are legally formed, financially structured, or protected. For many physicians, this creates unnecessary anxiety. Not because the concepts are impossible to understand, but because they feel foreign and consequential.

This section exists to bring clarity to that uncertainty.

The financial and legal foundations of your practice are not about optimization or growth. They're about structure, protection, and sustainability. These decisions create the framework within which everything else operates, including how money flows, how risk is managed, and how responsibility is defined.

When these foundations are unclear or rushed, even well-designed practices can feel unstable. When they're thoughtfully established, they create a sense of steadiness that allows you to focus on medicine, leadership, and long-term vision.

This work doesn't require you to be an expert in finance or law. It requires understanding the purpose of each decision, knowing what needs attention now versus later, and recognizing when to seek professional guidance.

Section III is not about doing everything at once. It's about putting the right pieces in place, in the right order, so your practice can operate with clarity and confidence from the beginning.

When the Idea Finally Becomes Real

There's a moment I've come to recognize almost immediately when it happens.

It usually comes near the end of a one-hour business plan review. The physician on the other side of the screen has taken my Plan to Practice Digital Course and is walking me through their plan, explaining what they want to build and why they're not completely sure if it will work.

They often start the call nervous. Beforehand, many of them tell me they felt overwhelmed while working through the business plan. Not because it was too complicated, but because it forced them to slow down and look directly at the details they'd been avoiding. The numbers. The expenses. The timeline. The uncertainty.

For weeks or months, the idea of private practice had lived mostly in their head. It felt exciting but abstract. Possible but fragile. Easy to poke holes in. Easy to dismiss on hard days.

Putting it on paper changed that.

During the review, we don't talk about perfection. We talk about assumptions. We walk through revenue, expenses, and early projections. We look at it not simply as predictions but as possibilities grounded in reality. We look at what makes sense and what needs adjustment. We identify what's solid and what's still evolving.

And then it happens. They pause. They look back at the plan and their tone shifts.

Often, they say something like, *I didn't realize this could actually work*, or *Seeing it laid out like this makes it feel real.*

That's the moment I'm waiting for.

Nothing magical has changed in that hour. But the fear has softened because now there's structure. The idea isn't floating anymore. It has shape, it has logic, and it has a path.

What surprises many physicians is how reassuring the business plan feels once it exists. They expected it to expose flaws or tell them they were being unrealistic. Instead, it gives them language, clarity, and something they can return to when doubt creeps in.

They don't necessarily leave the review feeling like expert business owners. But they do leave feeling grounded. And because they've already explained it to themselves, and to me, they can also explain their practice out loud to a potential partner or lender. They understand what they're building, what it will take, and what needs to happen next.

That's the real value of a business plan. It's not about approval or permission. It's about moving from, *I think this could work* to *I can see how this works.*

And once that shift happens, everything that follows feels less intimidating, including financial planning, legal review, and advisor conversations. The practice stops being a vague dream and starts becoming a thoughtful, intentional plan.

That's when private practice becomes real.

CHAPTER 11

The Business Plan Is a Blueprint, Not a Barrier

Most physicians think a business plan is just something they need for the bank. It's often viewed as a formal document and can seem intimidating, complicated, and easy to get wrong. Many physicians either avoid creating a business plan altogether or rush through it just to check a box.

That framing misses the real purpose of a business plan. In reality, a business plan exists to help you create a blueprint for the practice you plan to build. It's a space to get your ideas out of your head and onto paper. A space to think through what you're actually trying to create before you invest time, money, and energy.

A business plan is not a test, it's a thinking tool. This is where you begin to clarify who you want to serve, what services you plan to offer, how revenue will be generated, what expenses you should expect, and what success looks like in the early stages of your practice.

When physicians struggle with business plans, it's usually not because the concepts are too advanced. It's because they don't know where to start.

Many get stuck staring at a blank page, unsure of what's expected of them. Others freeze because they believe the plan has to be perfect or that once it's written, it's final. And almost everyone gets hung up when it comes to financial projections, especially if they haven't yet taken the time to understand what the math actually needs to look like.

Here's what's important to understand: Your business plan is allowed to change. It is not a contract, it's a working document. You can revisit it, refine it, and adjust it as you learn more. In fact, you should expect to do exactly that.

When physicians skip this step, or rush through it without clarity, the consequences tend to show up later. Unrealistic financial projections can lead to cash flow problems. Vague planning can result in a practice without a clear identity, making it harder to make decisions or explain what you're building to others.

A good business plan should clearly answer a few core questions: who you serve, what services you'll provide, how you plan to make money, what it will cost to operate, and what success looks like at the beginning.

You are allowed to dream big when creating your business plan. Vision belongs here. But dreaming big works best when paired with realism.

The purpose of a business plan isn't to predict the future or prove that you have everything figured out. It's a thinking tool, one that helps you slow down, examine your assumptions, and make intentional decisions about the practice you're building. When used this way, a business plan doesn't limit you. It gives you clarity, context, and a steadier foundation for the financial and legal decisions that follow.

CHAPTER 12

Making Sense of the Numbers

Most physicians assume that figuring out the math for a private practice requires an accountant.

And while accountants are incredibly helpful, you also have to understand the numbers when it comes to building your private practice. Too often, physicians outsource understanding because they believe the math will be too complicated or intimidating.

But the math exists for one simple reason: to make sure you're actually building a profitable practice. If you want to make a profit, what you bring in, your revenue, has to be more than what you send out, your expenses.

Where physicians get tripped up is not the equation, but the assumptions behind it. Most physicians can follow the math. What's harder is questioning the expectations embedded within those numbers, assumptions about how full a schedule should be, what patients will pay, how quickly growth should happen, and what sustainability actually looks like in practice.

The most dangerous mistakes in early projections include underestimating expenses, overestimating revenue, not understanding break-even, and not planning owner pay. Startup costs are often underestimated or inflated. Monthly expenses are glossed over. Revenue is projected as if the practice will be at full capacity immediately. Growth over time is ignored. When those assumptions go unexamined, the numbers can feel discouraging or restrictive, even when the math itself is sound.

The best place to start the math is not with expenses, it's with your take-home goal. A major oversight is failing to plan intentionally for personal income. Saying, *I'll take what's left*, may sound flexible, but it creates instability. Paying yourself should be part of the structure, not a reward.

From there, you work backward. How much revenue is required? What expenses are realistic? How many patients, visits, or memberships does that require? How many days and hours does that translate to?

That's what it means to *make the math math*. You are allowed to get it wrong the first time. You are allowed to revise. You are allowed to start over as many times as needed until the numbers reflect reality.

CHAPTER 13

Putting the Right Protections in Place

This is the part of building a private practice that many physicians would rather postpone. Not because it's unimportant, but because it feels unfamiliar, technical, and high-stakes. Legal structure, tax considerations, malpractice insurance, and compliance rarely show up in medical training, yet they carry real consequences when they're overlooked.

Putting the right protections in place is not about perfection or fear. It's about creating a practice that isn't fragile, one that can absorb mistakes, manage risk, and support you as an owner over time. These decisions form the guardrails of your practice. They don't make it rigid, they make it resilient.

Legal Structure

The legal structure of your practice defines where responsibility lives.

At its core, this decision is about separating your personal life from your professional one. A thoughtful legal structure creates clarity around ownership, liability, and decision-making. It establishes a boundary between you and the business in order to protect both.

The legal structure exists to reduce risk, create order, and provide a framework within which your practice can operate safely. When structure is ignored or rushed, physicians often don't realize the consequences until something goes wrong. When it's handled intentionally, it fades into the background, quietly doing its job. That's the goal.

Tax Structure

Tax structure is not about gaming the system or finding loopholes. It's about understanding how money moves through your practice and how different decisions affect what you keep, what you owe, and what you can plan for. You don't need to become a tax expert. You do need to understand that early decisions echo forward and guessing here can be expensive.

Clarity around tax structure doesn't come from mastering every rule. It comes from knowing enough to ask good questions and involving the right professionals before patterns are set in motion.

Malpractice Insurance and Compliance

Malpractice insurance and compliance requirements are often framed as burdens. In reality, they exist to protect the practice you're building and the people within it.

Malpractice coverage is not just a formality. It's a safeguard against the reality that medicine carries risk, even when practiced thoughtfully and well. Compliance requirements, while sometimes frustrating, serve a similar purpose. They establish standards, reduce exposure, and create consistency.

Approached reactively, these areas feel overwhelming. Approached intentionally, they provide peace of mind.

You don't have to set out to eliminate risk entirely, that's impossible. But you must make sure that a single issue doesn't unravel everything you've worked to build.

You Are Not Meant to Do This Alone

One of the most important mindset shifts in private practice ownership is recognizing that delegation is not avoidance, it's leadership.

Physicians are trained to take responsibility. That instinct is valuable, but it doesn't mean you're meant to personally manage every legal, financial, or compliance decision. The right protections are rarely built in isolation. They're built with support.

This is where advisors come in. Advisors should not serve to take control away from you, but to help you make informed decisions within your vision. Legal counsel, accounting support, and insurance professionals exist to prevent mistakes that are difficult or costly to undo later. Choosing to involve them is not a sign that you're unprepared. It's a sign that you understand the weight of ownership.

Putting the right protections in place doesn't make your practice complicated. It makes it stable. And stability is what allows everything else, including growth, flexibility, and sustainability, to follow.

CHAPTER 14

Reviewing Your Current Employment Contract

The decision to leave employment and build a private practice doesn't start with a resignation letter. It starts with understanding the agreements that currently govern your employment. Before you form an entity, choose insurance, or finalize the structure of your future practice, there's one step that deserves early attention, and that's reviewing your employment contract.

Employment contracts shape how, when, and where you're allowed to practice medicine, sometimes long after you've given your notice. Reviewing yours early is not about fear or confrontation. It's about clarity. It allows you to plan responsibly and put the right protections in place before you take the next steps.

Most physicians avoid reviewing their employment contract because they don't fully understand it or because they fear what they might find. But avoiding the contract doesn't make its terms disappear. Employment contracts often include clauses that can directly affect your ability to open a practice, including non-competes, notice periods, patient-related restrictions, intellectual property language, and termination terms.

A commonly overlooked section in the employment contract involves malpractice coverage. Your contract outlines what happens to malpractice insurance after you leave, including whether tail coverage is required and who is responsible for it. This can carry significant financial implications if not planned for ahead of time.

The biggest risk of not reviewing your contract early is discovering too late that it affects where, when, or how you can open your practice. Because of the high stakes, this is not something to navigate alone. Legal review by an attorney experienced with physician contracts is a protective step, not a confrontational one.

Reviewing your employment contract early is not about anticipating conflict. It's about reducing uncertainty during a transition that already carries enough weight. When you understand your restrictions, timelines, and obligations, you're able to plan the next steps of your practice with clarity instead of assumption.

This kind of foresight doesn't slow progress, it protects it and allows you to move forward with confidence as you build what comes next.

CHAPTER 15

Creating Financial Stability Early

The early financial phase of private practice can feel more fragile than physicians expect. Revenue may be inconsistent at first, but expenses arrive on schedule whether patients do or not. And even when the practice is technically "profitable," it can still feel stressful to manage day to day. This is not a sign that something is wrong, it's a normal part of building something new.

What determines whether this phase feels manageable or chaotic is rarely volume alone, it's discipline. Early financial stability isn't about having perfect numbers or rapid growth. It's about creating enough structure to understand what's happening, maintain boundaries, and make decisions from a place of clarity rather than urgency.

Cash Flow: Timing Matters More Than Totals

Many physicians focus on whether the practice will be profitable, but profitability and cash flow are not the same thing.

Cash flow is about timing. It reflects when money comes in, when expenses go out, and how predictable that rhythm is. Rent, payroll, and vendors don't wait for claims to process or payments to settle. When timing isn't well understood, even a healthy practice can feel perpetually behind. Without a clear sense of when revenue arrives relative to expenses, decisions start to feel reactive. Stability comes from understanding that rhythm early and planning around it. Clarity here doesn't require complex forecasting, it requires awareness.

Separating Business and Personal Finances: A Boundary That Matters

One of the most common early mistakes in private practice is treating business and personal finances interchangeably.

This often starts innocently. Maybe you find yourself covering a shortfall, reimbursing yourself informally, or paying a business expense personally "just this once." Over time, those small exceptions blur important boundaries.

Separating finances is not just a formality. It protects your legal structure, preserves clarity around what the practice can actually support, and reduces emotional decision-making. When boundaries are clear, it's easier to assess performance honestly and plan responsibly. Blurring those lines doesn't just create accounting headaches, it makes it harder to lead.

Tracking: Consistency Over Complexity

Financial tracking doesn't need to be perfect to be effective. Early on, the goal is not sophisticated reporting or deep analysis. The goal is consistency: knowing where money is going, noticing patterns, and catching problems before they compound.

Inconsistent tracking creates blind spots. It makes small issues harder to spot and larger ones more stressful to address. Regular awareness, even at a high level, builds confidence and reduces uncertainty.

There are many software options available for tracking, or you may choose to employ a bookkeeper. A steady rhythm of review matters more than the tool you use. Tracking your finances is about developing a leadership habit.

Stability Comes From Structure

Taken together, these practices create something essential: steadiness.

Early financial stability doesn't come from avoiding challenges. It comes from meeting them with structure, boundaries, and visibility. These systems don't eliminate uncertainty, but they reduce its impact.

Creating stability early protects momentum. It gives your practice room to grow without unnecessary strain. And it reinforces one of the most important lessons of ownership: Calm doesn't come from certainty, it comes from preparation.

57

This section was about stability.

The financial and legal foundations you've considered here are meant to support the practice you're building. With these pieces in place, you're building from a position of clarity and protection.

Section IV: Building the Practice Infrastructure

At some point, clarity has to turn into action.

By the time you reach this section, you've done important work. You've examined your assumptions. You've defined your mission. You've made intentional choices about your practice model, services, schedule, and finances. Now the question becomes practical: How do you turn all of that into something real?

This is where many physicians feel the pressure to get everything exactly right.

Infrastructure decisions feel permanent. A location. A layout. Technology. Systems. These choices can feel heavy because they come with contracts, costs, and the fear of making the "wrong" decision. It's easy to believe that if you don't choose perfectly now, you'll be stuck later.

Section IV exists to reframe that pressure.

Infrastructure is not about perfection. It's about creating something functional enough to begin. Most early decisions are not permanent, they're simply starting points. What matters most is that what you build supports patient care, allows your practice to operate smoothly, and leaves room for growth.

This section will help you think clearly about the physical and operational pieces of your practice without letting fear or overthinking stall progress. The goal is not to eliminate uncertainty. It's to move forward thoughtfully, with enough structure to support you and enough flexibility to adapt.

A Place to Begin

When physicians reach the stage of building their practice infrastructure, the anxiety often changes.

Earlier fears tend to be about whether private practice is possible. At this point, the fear is different. It's about permanence. Location, layout, technology, and workflow. Each decision can start to feel final, as though one wrong choice could derail everything before it even begins.

Because of that, many physicians slow down here. Not because they lack motivation, but because they're trying to get it right.

I see this most often in thoughtful, capable physicians who care deeply about building something solid. They research extensively. They compare options. They imagine future scenarios and try to account for all of them in advance. They want the space to be perfect, the systems to be future-proof, and the workflow to anticipate every possible situation.

This stalls progress. What's usually missing isn't information, it's permission.

Permission to start without everything being finished. Permission to choose something that works *for now*. Permission to treat early decisions as adjustable rather than permanent.

One physician I worked with described feeling stuck for months, unable to move forward because every decision felt irreversible. Choosing a location felt like choosing her professional fate. Picking technology felt like a lifelong commitment. Even layout decisions carried emotional weight. What shifted things for her wasn't finding the perfect answer, it was realizing that very few early infrastructure decisions are truly permanent. Practices move. Layouts change. Technology evolves. Workflows improve once real patients walk through the door.

Once she stopped asking, *Is this the best possible choice?* and started asking, *Will this work well enough to begin?* momentum returned. Decisions became lighter. Progress resumed. The practice started to take shape, not as a final version, but as a starting point.

And this isn't just something I've observed in others.

In my own practice, our first location wasn't ideal. It worked well enough to get us started, but within the first year, it was clear that the practice had grown beyond what that space could support. So we adjusted. I purchased a new space and built a clinic that better fit what the practice was becoming.

A few years later, as our staff grew, we made changes again to support that growth. By year three, it became obvious that our phone system could no longer handle the volume and complexity of what we'd built, so we overhauled it.

None of those changes meant we had made mistakes early on. They meant the practice was evolving. Each adjustment was a response to growth, not a correction of failure.

That's the reframe most physicians need at this stage. You are not building the final version of your practice here. You are building a place to begin. When infrastructure decisions are approached with that mindset, perfectionism loosens its grip. Overspending becomes less tempting. Fear gives way to thoughtful action. The practice begins to feel real. Not because everything is finished, but because it's finally moving.

This section isn't about locking yourself into choices you can't undo. It's about making grounded decisions that support good care, reasonable days, and a sustainable path forward.

From here, building becomes possible. When you reach this point, it's no longer about getting everything right, it's about getting started.

CHAPTER 16

Choosing a Location

Most physicians get stuck when it comes to choosing a location.

They assume they need to find the perfect place, the space they'll be in for the rest of their career. Because of that belief, they spend an enormous amount of time trying to get this decision exactly right. The pressure builds, momentum slows, and what should be a forward-moving step turns into a major obstacle.

One common assumption is that location alone will determine success. While it's true that you want a space that's reasonably easy for patients to find, the reality is that patients are capable. They use Google and GPS. They can find you in far more places than we sometimes give them credit for. Of course, this doesn't mean location doesn't matter at all. You don't want to be in an area that feels unsafe or uncomfortable. But beyond basic safety and accessibility, your location is what *you* make it.

Another belief that trips physicians up is the idea that they only get one chance. That if they choose the "wrong" location, the practice is somehow doomed.

That simply isn't true.

Many practices move at some point, for various reasons. Maybe it's because they need more space, because the original layout no longer fits, or because the practice has evolved. Your first location does not have to be your forever location. It just needs to work for the season you're in now.

What actually matters most when choosing a location is fairly straightforward. You need enough space to practice efficiently. The area should feel safe for you, your staff, and your patients. And it should be a place you're proud to put your name on and share with the community.

It's important to understand that you are allowed to consider multiple options when choosing a location. Some physicians start with a blank canvas and build it out. Others choose spaces previously used as medical offices. Neither approach is inherently better. What matters is that the space fits your needs, your budget, and your current stage. Mistakes tend to happen when physicians choose location based on ego rather than intention. Overspending is common, especially when trying to replicate the footprint of larger, established practices. High monthly lease or mortgage costs can quietly add financial pressure to the practice early on.

Choosing a location doesn't have to be paralyzing. You're not locking yourself into a lifetime decision, you're choosing a place to begin.

CHAPTER 17

Designing the Clinic Layout

Most physicians struggle with finalizing their clinic layout.

This usually shows up as copying what they've seen before at large health systems, previous employers, or clinics that look impressive on paper, without stopping to consider that this is *their* space. While there are compliance requirements every clinic must meet, much of the layout is far more flexible than physicians often realize.

A common pitfall is prioritizing aesthetics over function. It's easy to design a beautiful space that photographs well but doesn't work smoothly day to day. While your clinic should feel welcoming, function has to come first. A layout that supports efficiency, for you and for your staff, will matter far more than design choices meant only to impress.

At its core, your clinic layout should support flow. You need enough exam rooms to match your schedule, adequate bathrooms, ADA accessibility, and a layout that allows patients and staff to move through the space comfortably. Everything else is secondary to how the day actually functions.

Early on, many physicians assume every room needs to be fully equipped from day one. In reality, you only need enough to begin seeing patients safely and effectively. Additional equipment, furnishings, and upgrades can be added as the practice grows and your needs become clearer.

Patients often notice far less than we think. Most patients are looking for a good doctor, a smooth visit, and a space that feels professional and comfortable.

They are not auditing your layout. When physicians let go of the pressure to get everything perfect immediately, layout decisions become much simpler.

When considering the layout, remember that the waiting room is the physical gateway to your practice and should be welcoming. One choice I strongly encourage physicians to consider is having a private office for themselves. This is a practice you are intentionally building. A space for focused work, privacy, and reflection supports longevity, especially as your role shifts between clinician and owner. Even a modest personal office can make a meaningful difference in how sustainable your days feel. Your staff also need space that works for them. They need a place to do their work efficiently, and you should provide this for them. Whether you include other spaces like a triage room, lab, or additional areas should be driven entirely by the services you plan to offer.

Simplicity early on is often an advantage. Clinics evolve and layouts change. What matters most is that your space allows you to care for patients well today, while leaving room to adjust tomorrow.

Your first layout does not need to reflect the final version of your practice. It needs to support good care, a functional day, and a practice you can continue shaping over time. Designing your clinic is not about getting everything right at once. It's about building something that works well enough to begin, and flexible enough to grow with you.

CHAPTER 18

Choosing Technology That Supports Your Practice

Technology decisions are some of the most consequential choices you'll make early in private practice. This isn't because the technology choices you make need to be perfect, but because they shape how your days in your practice will actually function.

Many physicians approach technology with hesitation. They worry about choosing the wrong system, overspending, or getting locked into tools that create more frustration than efficiency. That fear often leads to one of two extremes: over-researching every option until progress stalls, or outsourcing decisions entirely and hoping things work themselves out. Neither approach serves you well.

Technology is not about having the most advanced tools. It's about building systems that support how you practice medicine. Early on, technology should be thought of as infrastructure. This applies to everyday essentials: computers, printers, scanners, phone systems, communication platforms, etc. Just like your location and layout, your technology choices need to support flow, efficiency, and reliability. These tools quietly determine how information moves through your practice, how staff communicate, and how much friction exists in your day.

One of the biggest mistakes physicians make is choosing tools in isolation. An EHR that doesn't integrate with your billing system. A phone platform that doesn't allow for easy routing of calls. A patient communication tool that creates extra steps instead of simplifying them. Individually, each choice may seem reasonable. Together, they create inefficiency and frustration that compound over time.

The goal is not complexity. The goal is integration.

Early technology decisions should be evaluated through a simple lens:

Does this make my day easier?

Does it reduce steps, not add them?

Does it work well with the other systems I'm using?

Is it reliable, teachable, and supported?

Does the cost make sense for where my practice is right now?

Technology should adapt to your workflow, not force you to change how you practice in order to accommodate it.

Technology decisions are not permanent. Systems can be changed, upgraded, or replaced as your practice grows. But that doesn't mean early choices don't matter. Poorly chosen tools can drain time, energy, and morale. Thoughtful choices create breathing room and consistency, especially during the already demanding early months of ownership.

You don't need every feature. You don't need every integration. You don't need to future-proof everything. You need tools that work consistently, are easy for your staff to learn, and support patient care without becoming the center of your attention.

If technology is not your comfort zone, that's okay. You are not expected to be an expert. You are expected to be intentional. Asking questions, requesting demos, and understanding how systems connect is part of ownership. Don't perceive having to ask questions as a personal shortcoming; understanding the technology systems you are investing in is your duty as the practice owner.

One technology decision deserves special attention because of how central it becomes to daily life in medical practice. That system is your electronic health record. And because of its impact on workflow, efficiency, and patient care, it deserves a chapter of its own.

CHAPTER 19

Committing to an EHR

If there is one technology decision that shapes daily life in your practice more than any other, it is your electronic health record.

Your EHR becomes the system everything else revolves around. It influences how quickly you move through your day, how information flows between staff, how patients experience your practice, and how efficiently care is delivered. Unlike many other tools, it is not something you interact with occasionally. You use it constantly. Because of that, choosing an EHR deserves more time and attention than most physicians initially expect.

Many physicians approach this decision hoping there is a single "best" option. There isn't. Every EHR comes with strengths, limitations, and tradeoffs. The right system is not the most popular one, the most expensive one, or the one with the longest feature list. It is the one that fits how *you* practice medicine and how *your* clinic needs to function day to day.

This is why comparison matters. Choosing an EHR should never be a one-demo decision. What looks impressive in a sales presentation may feel very different during a busy clinic day. Features that sound helpful may add friction in real use. And systems that seem similar on the surface can feel dramatically different once you begin clicking through workflows.

Before making a decision, it's worth slowing down enough to compare multiple platforms side by side. As you evaluate options, think beyond appearance and marketing. Imagine your busiest clinic day. Picture yourself moving quickly between patients, reviewing labs, sending prescriptions, documenting visits, and responding to messages. Does the system support that pace or does it slow you down?

One step that often gets overlooked is talking to other physicians you trust, ideally in your specialty and in the same practice model, about the systems they use. Not just *what* they chose, but *why*. Ask what they like, what frustrates them, and how responsive customer support has been when things go wrong. These conversations often reveal things you won't learn in a demo.

Key factors to weigh include usability, speed, reliability, customer support, cost, and how well the system integrates with the other technology you've chosen. An EHR that doesn't communicate well with billing, scheduling, or patient communication tools can create inefficiency that compounds over time.

One of the most common mistakes physicians make is letting sales pressure rush this decision. EHR vendors are skilled at highlighting strengths and minimizing limitations. That's their job. Your job is to ask thoughtful questions, request realistic demos, and take the time you need to decide. Feeling hurried or uneasy during the process is often a sign that you need more information, not that you need to commit in a hurry.

It's also important to be honest about the reality of switching systems. While it is possible to change EHRs, it is not easy. Transitions require time, retraining, data migration, and significant emotional energy, for you and your staff. That doesn't mean you have to find a perfect system initially. But it does mean this decision deserves respect so that you can be confident you're making the best decision possible.

The goal is not to anticipate every EHR need you may have years from now. The goal is to choose a system you can work with consistently, efficiently, and confidently as you open your doors and grow.

If technology is not your comfort zone, you don't need to become an expert on EHR systems, but you do need to be engaged. Ask questions, take notes, compare experiences, and pay attention to what feels intuitive and what feels frustrating. Your daily experience matters more than any feature list.

An EHR is not just software. It becomes part of how you practice medicine. Choosing the right one is not about getting it "right" forever. It's about choosing intentionally, with clarity about how you want your practice to function from day one.

CHAPTER 20

Designing the Way Your Practice Flows

Workflow is where everything you've planned finally meets reality.

It's how work actually moves through your practice. It's how patients experience their visit, how staff experience their day, and how much energy you have left at the end of clinic. More than almost anything else, workflow determines whether a practice feels sustainable or exhausting.

When physicians talk about burnout in private practice, they're rarely talking about medicine itself. They're usually talking about days that feel chaotic: phones interrupting constantly, rooms not ready when they need them, patients waiting longer than expected, or charting that spills into evenings and weekends.

Those problems are rarely about effort, they're almost always about flow. Most physicians approach workflow by copying what they've seen before, recreating systems from previous jobs without questioning whether they actually worked.

It's important to remember that you are allowed to design the way your practice flows. Private practice gives you the freedom to take the best of what you've seen and leave the rest behind. If a previous clinic handled phone triage well, borrow that structure. If another had efficient rooming or clear handoffs, use what worked. And if certain systems consistently led to frustration, like constant interruptions, room delays, or documentation piling up after hours, know that you are not obligated to recreate them.

Workflow is not about proving how much you can handle. It's about creating a system that supports good care, consistently.

The efficiency of your workflow matters most for two groups: your staff and your patients. When workflow supports staff, their days feel clearer and more manageable. Roles are defined, handoffs make sense, and interruptions decrease. When it doesn't, even the hardest-working team ends the day drained and reactive.

Patients feel workflow too, even if they can't name it. They experience it in how long they wait, how smoothly the visit moves, and whether the visit feels organized or rushed. Door-to-door time is not about speed, it's about respect for their time and trust in your practice.

Keep in mind that workflow is not static.

You cannot design every detail on paper. Some inefficiencies will only become visible once patients are in the building and the day is unfolding in real time. Early friction does not mean failure, it means you're learning. Paying attention to where delays happen and where energy is lost gives you the information you need to improve.

Designing the way your practice flows is an ongoing act of leadership. It requires stepping back periodically to assess whether the systems you've built still support the kind of practice you want to run. Small adjustments can dramatically change how a day feels for you, your staff, and your patients.

A practice that flows well does not happen by accident. It happens when workflow is treated as something worth designing intentionally, thoughtfully, and with the understanding that how the day feels matters just as much as what gets done.

This section was about moving from intention to execution.

Not rushing decisions or eliminating uncertainty, but putting structure in place so uncertainty doesn't run the show. The choices you've considered here, including location, layout, technology, and workflow, are meant to support the practice as it begins to function in real time.

With these pieces in place, your practice is no longer just a plan on paper. You're building from a position of clarity rather than reaction.

Section V: Becoming Visible

By the time you reach this section, your practice exists, at least on paper.

You've made decisions about how you want to practice, what you're offering, how your days are structured, and what systems support your work. Now comes a part of private practice that many physicians feel uneasy about: visibility.

Marketing is often framed as something separate from good medicine or, worse, something that cheapens it. Many physicians worry that promoting their practice feels self-serving, uncomfortable, or in conflict with the values that drew them to medicine in the first place.

This section exists to reframe that narrative.

Helping patients find you is not about performance or persuasion. It's about clarity and connection. The right patients cannot choose your practice if they don't know you exist or don't understand what you offer.

Visibility doesn't require burnout. You don't need to be everywhere, you don't need to be loud, and you don't need to build your identity around marketing. You do need to be intentional.

This section will help you think through how patients actually find practices, how to communicate your message clearly, and how to show up consistently without exhausting yourself. The goal isn't growth at all costs, it's alignment.

Letting People Find Me

If you had asked me early on what I thought about marketing, I would have told you it wasn't really my thing.

I didn't go into medicine to promote myself. I wasn't interested in becoming an "online doctor," and I certainly didn't want to feel like I was selling something. In my mind, good medicine should speak for itself. If you provided excellent care, patients would find you.

That belief felt principled. It also felt safe.

But once I decided to open my own practice, I realized something quickly: Patients can't choose a practice they don't know exists.

At first, I hoped word of mouth would be enough. And while it mattered, a lot, it wasn't sufficient on its own.

What made marketing uncomfortable for me wasn't the work itself, it was the story I had attached to it. I had equated visibility with ego. I had assumed that showing up meant overselling, exaggerating, or becoming someone I wasn't.

So I avoided it.

When I finally did begin sharing about my practice, it felt awkward. At first, I second-guessed every post. I wondered if people thought I was doing too much or trying too hard. None of it felt natural. But over time, that consistent, values-driven approach led to a large following. Not because I set out to build a platform, but because I showed up and represented my clinic and brand in a way that felt honest and accessible.

And then something wonderful happened.

Patients began telling me they felt like they already knew me before they ever walked through the clinic door. They understood what my practice stood for. They knew what kind of care to expect. They felt reassured before they ever became patients.

That was when my thinking finally shifted.

Marketing, I realized, wasn't about convincing people to choose me. It was about giving the right people an opportunity to find me. It was about clarity, not performance. Connection, not persuasion.

Once I stopped trying to market like someone else and started showing up in ways that felt aligned with my values, my community, and my patients, everything changed. Visibility didn't require me to become louder or more polished. It required me to be present.

Marketing didn't change who I was as a physician. It simply allowed the people who needed me to find me.

CHAPTER 21

Marketing Is Not a Dirty Word

Most physicians resist marketing because they don't want to be salesy.

There's a deeply ingrained belief, perhaps shaped by training and reinforced by culture, that marketing isn't something doctors should do. Somewhere along the way, many physicians internalized the idea that good medicine should speak for itself, and that actively promoting a practice feels uncomfortable or even inappropriate.

Corporate medicine has only strengthened this belief. In large systems, physicians are rarely responsible for attracting patients. Marketing is handled at an institutional level, far removed from the exam room. Over time, this creates the impression that physicians shouldn't market, or that we don't need to. But private practice operates under a very different reality.

At its core, marketing is not selling. Marketing is simply how you introduce your practice to the world. It's how patients learn that you exist. It's how they understand who you help, what kind of care you provide, and whether your practice might be right for them. Marketing your practice isn't about convincing people to need something they don't. It's about making it easier for the right patients to find you.

One of the most common mistakes physicians make is assuming patients will just magically show up. Imagine me holding your hand when I say this: They won't.

Even excellent physicians with well-designed practices need a way to let people know they're there.

Here's the permission I want you to read clearly: You should feel comfortable expressing yourself when it comes to marketing your practice. You are allowed to talk about the care you provide. You are allowed to share why you built your practice the way you did. You are allowed to let people know you're open and ready to serve them.

The goal of marketing isn't perfection. The goal is getting people in the door. Marketing doesn't change who you are as a physician. It simply allows your work, your values, and your practice to be visible to the people who need it. When done thoughtfully, it becomes an extension of care, not a departure from it.

CHAPTER 22

Getting Clear on Your Message

Most physicians overthink their message because they believe it has to be perfect and that it has to appeal to everyone.

Neither of those beliefs is true, and that pressure often leads to over-explaining. Physicians try to include every service they offer, every condition they treat, and every possible patient they could help. The result is a message that is technically accurate but emotionally flat and difficult for patients to connect with.

A common assumption is that your wording has to be polished, rehearsed, and final before you can share it. Another is that you need to explain everything about your practice upfront. Neither of those things is true.

Patients aren't looking for perfection. They're looking for clarity.

A clear message tells patients how you and your practice can impact their health and their lives. It helps them understand whether what you offer fits what they need. It doesn't try to convince everyone, it helps the *right* people recognize themselves. Physicians sometimes default to institutional language and use phrases that sound like a hospital website instead of a human being. But patients connect with people, not systems. They want to know who you are, what you value, and what they can expect when they walk through your doors.

Your message should reflect the kind of care you plan to provide. It should align with your mission, your services, and the patient population you've intentionally chosen. When those pieces are aligned, messaging becomes simpler and far more effective.

Here's the permission many physicians need in this phase: You are allowed to brag on yourself and your practice when defining your message. That doesn't mean exaggerating or posturing. It means clearly and confidently communicating what you do well and why your approach matters. You've trained for this. You've been thoughtful about what you're building. Patients deserve to hear that.

Your message doesn't have to be perfect to be shared. It just needs to be clear, honest, and consistent.

CHAPTER 23

Referral Partners Still Matter

Most physicians underestimate referral partners because they don't realize how important those relationships are to building a successful practice.

In employed medicine, especially within large systems, referrals often feel automatic. Patients flow in through institutional pathways and physicians rarely have to think about where those patients came from or why. As a result, referral-building can feel unfamiliar or even unnecessary when transitioning to private practice.

But private practice works differently.

Whether your practice is insurance-based or cash-pay, referral relationships are a foundational part of growth. Patients don't just appear. They're often directed, encouraged, and reassured by people they already trust.

At its core, referral-building is about relationships and trust. It's about helping other professionals understand who you serve, what kind of care you provide, and when it makes sense to send someone your way. When referral partners clearly understand what you offer, they can confidently recommend your practice to the right patients.

One of the most common mistakes physicians make is assuming referrals will happen organically. They rarely do. Securing referrals requires consistent effort and time.

Another common issue is not being able to clearly explain the practice to referral sources. If you can't easily describe who your practice is for and how you help patients, it becomes harder for others to refer appropriately. Referrals also stall when physicians reach out once and then stop. Building referral relationships requires consistency, not a single conversation.

Referral partners are broader than many physicians realize. Yes, other physicians matter, primary care, specialists, and colleagues in adjacent fields. But non-physician referral sources are equally important. Therapists, counselors, physical therapists, gyms, schools, churches, community organizations, and local businesses often have direct relationships with the patients you're trying to serve. You should aim to reach out to them as well as to other physicians.

Building referral relationships doesn't require formal presentations or polished pitches. It requires clarity, follow-through, and genuine connection. You don't need to sound scripted or corporate. You don't need to "sell" yourself. You simply need to explain what you do, who you help, and why your practice exists. Being approachable and consistent goes much further than being impressive.

Building referral relationships is not about asking for favors. It's about creating connections that help patients get the care they need.

CHAPTER 24

Showing Up Online

I want to be honest with you, social media mattered a lot when I launched my practice.

Before opening, I was intentional about how I showed up online. I didn't try to be everywhere. I didn't post constantly. I chose one primary platform, Facebook, and I used it strategically.

When I shared my first post announcing the practice, it was shared more than 700 times.

If you assume the average person has around 300 Facebook friends, that means over 200,000 people learned about my practice through that single post. That reach didn't happen by accident. It happened because I was clear, intentional, and willing to show up.

That experience reshaped how I think about online presence for private practice.

Being online isn't about chasing trends or becoming an influencer, it's about visibility. Patients can't find what they don't know exists. And in today's world, many patients first "meet" a practice online long before they ever walk through the door.

One of the biggest mistakes I see physicians make is assuming they don't need to be online, or that having a basic listing somewhere is enough. It's not. Another is believing they need to be on every platform to be successful. You don't. But you *do* need to be strategic.

That means choosing a platform you're comfortable with and showing up there consistently. For some physicians, that's Facebook. For others, it might be Instagram, LinkedIn, or another platform entirely. The goal isn't to do everything, it's to do something well enough that people know you exist and understand what you offer.

Online presence isn't about perfection. It's about clarity and consistency.

Your posts don't need to be polished and your videos don't need to be professionally planned and edited. You just need to show up.

When we talk about showing up online, your website plays a role here too. Think of your website as your digital home base. It's often where patients go after hearing about you online or from a referral partner. A well-built website should clearly explain who you serve, what services you offer, how to contact you, and what makes your practice different. It doesn't need to be flashy, but it does need to be clear. I encourage physicians to invest thoughtfully in their website early on. This is one place where doing it well from the start pays dividends. Patients should be able to understand your practice within minutes, not have to hunt for basic information.

Showing up online is not about saying everything or being everywhere. It's about being present in a way that feels sustainable, honest, and aligned with the practice you're building.

CHAPTER 25

Consistency Beats Complexity

When physicians think about marketing their practice, many assume success comes from doing more. More platforms. More posts. More strategies. More effort. That belief often leads to burnout before momentum ever has a chance to build. In reality, complexity rarely creates growth, consistency does.

One of the biggest misconceptions in practice marketing is the idea that you need to do everything at once. Physicians try to maintain multiple platforms, test different strategies, and chase every new idea they hear, often without giving any single approach enough time to work.

The result is frustration, not traction. Patients don't find practices because they saw one perfect post. They find practices because they see them repeatedly, over time, in ways that feel familiar and trustworthy. Consistency builds recognition. Recognition builds trust. Trust leads to patients.

A simple, repeatable approach almost always outperforms an elaborate one that's hard to sustain. This applies to everything you've considered in this section: showing up online, communicating your message, and building referral relationships. Doing one or two things well, and doing them consistently, matters far more than trying to do everything once.

Consistency doesn't make your practice boring. It makes it reliable. For patients, reliability builds trust. For you, it builds momentum. And for your practice, it creates a presence that feels steady rather than scattered.

This section was about presence.

Not promotion or performance, but helping the right people come to know who you are and how you practice. The marketing choices you've considered here are not meant to make your practice louder. They are meant to make it clearer.

Consistently showing up, through your message, your relationships, and your presence, allows your practice to grow in a way that feels steady rather than forced.

Section VI: Building the Team That Supports the Practice

At some point, private practice stops being a solo effort.

Up until now, much of what you've done has centered on you. Your vision, your decisions, and your willingness to step into ownership. But no practice grows, stabilizes, or sustains itself on one person alone. And trying to do everything yourself is one of the fastest ways to recreate the exhaustion you were hoping to leave behind.

For many physicians, building a team is one of the most intimidating parts of private practice.

Hiring feels unfamiliar. Managing people feels too personal. The responsibility can feel heavy, especially when you realize that your decisions affect not just patients, but the livelihoods of the people you bring into your practice. It's common to worry about making the wrong choice, disappointing someone, or having to navigate conflict you were never trained for.

Because of that fear, some physicians delay hiring longer than they should. Others hire quickly without clarity, hoping things will "work themselves out." Neither approach serves you, or the practice, well.

One of the most common misconceptions about building a team is that you need to hire several people at once. In reality, many practices begin much leaner than physicians expect and then expand intentionally as volume and complexity increase. Starting smaller allows you to learn what your practice actually needs instead of staffing for a hypothetical future version. It keeps early expenses manageable, clarifies workflows, and makes it easier to identify when adding another person truly makes sense.

There is no universal staffing formula. The "right" starting team depends on your services, your schedule, your patient volume, and how much administrative work you're willing to carry early on. What matters most is clarity, not size.

This section is about approaching team-building with the same intention you've applied everywhere else.

You don't need to become an HR expert. You don't need perfect systems. And you don't need to get everything right the first time. What you do need is a shift in how you think about hiring, onboarding, culture, and delegation.

Your team is not just support for the practice, they are part of the practice. When built thoughtfully, the right team protects your energy, strengthens patient care, and allows you to step fully into your role as both physician and owner. This section will help you move from doing everything yourself to building something that can truly sustain you and your future practice.

The Cost of Carrying It All

In addition to helping physicians launch their practices, I also have the privilege of working with many physicians who already have private practices but feel stuck, and there's a pattern I see again and again.

It usually starts with a capable, thoughtful physician who is doing a lot of things right. They've clarified their vision. They care deeply about their patients. They're committed to building something sustainable. But when the conversation turns to hiring, the energy shifts.

They hesitate.

Often, they tell me they're just being cautious. They want to make sure they hire the right person. They worry about bringing someone else on too soon or making the wrong choice. Managing people feels unfamiliar and the responsibility feels heavy. So they decide to wait.

In the meantime, they carry more. They return phone calls between patients. They handle scheduling issues themselves. They manage bills, triage messages, and solve problems as they come up. They tell themselves this is temporary and that once things settle down, they'll hire.

At first, it works. But over time, the practice begins to lean entirely on them. Their days become fragmented by constant interruptions. Focus is hard to maintain. Fatigue creeps in. Not just physical tiredness, but the kind of fatigue that comes from never fully stepping out of problem-solving mode.

When these physicians describe their days to me, they often sound puzzled. They're doing meaningful work. The practice is growing. And yet, they're exhausted.

As I listen, I often find myself thinking the same thing: They don't need a major overhaul, they need one more person. Not because they're failing. Not because they've built something wrong. But because no practice that requires efficiency and financial sustainability can rest entirely on one person's shoulders.

What's interesting is that when we talk about adding someone to the team, the first question is almost always about cost. How much will it cost to hire another person? Can the practice afford it?

But the cost that rarely gets attention is the cost of not hiring. The cost of lost focus. The cost of constant interruptions. The cost of carrying tasks that don't require a physician's training. The cost of mental fatigue that follows them home at the end of the day. In practices where efficiency matters, and where the physician wants to build something that lasts, those hidden costs add up quickly.

The shift doesn't happen when someone suddenly feels confident about hiring. It happens when they realize that doing everything themselves isn't protecting the practice, it's quietly draining it. And that's when asking for help begins to look less like a risk and more like a necessary step forward.

CHAPTER 26

Hiring Is a Skill You Learn

Most physicians struggle with hiring because they've never had to do it before and they're afraid of making the wrong decision.

In medicine, we aren't trained to hire. We're trained to diagnose, treat, and make high-stakes decisions quickly. Hiring feels different. It's personal. It carries weight. And for many physicians, it brings up fears they've never had to confront professionally.

That fear usually isn't about resumes or interviews. It's about responsibility.

When you hire someone, you're responsible for their livelihood. Their paycheck matters to their family. Their experience working for you becomes part of your reputation. And early on, your staff are a direct reflection of what you're building. That can feel heavy, especially when you're just getting started.

Another layer of fear is the possibility of having to let someone go. Most physicians are deeply uncomfortable with conflict, and termination feels like a personal failure rather than a business decision. That fear alone keeps many doctors stuck, understaffed, or doing far too much themselves.

The result is often hesitation or even rushing. Some physicians delay hiring longer than they should because they're afraid to commit. Others hire too quickly just to relieve pressure, without slowing down to make sure the fit is right.

The most common mistakes I see with early hires aren't about bad intentions, they're about process. Physicians often skip due diligence because they don't know what to look for. They hire based on credentials alone, they aren't clear upfront about expectations, or they assume someone will "figure it out" without structured training.

And one mistake shows up more than almost any other: not hiring for culture fit.

In early hiring, culture fit matters perhaps more than skill. Skills can be taught. Systems can be learned. But attitude, adaptability, and alignment with what you're building are much harder to change. Early staff help shape the tone of the practice, including how patients feel, how problems are handled, and how the day flows.

Don't get me wrong, that doesn't mean you should ignore competence. It means you shouldn't sacrifice fit for the sake of filling a role quickly.

Hiring takes time. Thoughtful hiring takes intention.

When you begin the process of hiring, remember: You are allowed to consider multiple people. You are allowed to say no. You are allowed to turn people down even if they seem "good enough." You do not have to hire the first person you meet, and you are not failing if you realize someone isn't the right fit and choose to keep looking.

Hiring is not a personality trait. It's not something you're either good at or bad at. Hiring is a skill. And like every other skill in medicine, it gets better with practice.

Hiring is only the beginning. What matters most is how you support, train, and lead the people you bring into your practice.

CHAPTER 27

Onboarding and Training Matter

Most physicians underinvest in onboarding and training because they're not sure how to do it.

More specifically, they're not sure how to train people in roles they've never personally held. You may not know exactly what it's like to work the front desk all day, manage phone calls, or handle nursing workflows minute by minute. And because those aren't roles you've lived in, training can feel overwhelming or unclear.

But here's the shift that matters: Even if those aren't your roles, you are now the CEO of the practice. And as the owner, onboarding and training are part of your responsibility. Early training is where you begin shaping the culture of the practice you're building.

Many physicians are used to learning on the fly. We adapted during training because we had to, and it can be tempting to assume new staff in your practice will do the same. But relying on that approach in your own practice often leads to inefficiency, confusion, and frustration.

Training and onboarding deserve to be taken seriously because they set the tone. Ideally, most onboarding and training should happen *before* the practice ever opens its doors. That early window is when you have the most control over systems, expectations, and pace. At the same time, it's important to recognize that training doesn't end on opening day. Once patients start coming in, you'll notice things that need to be adjusted.

Training often feels overwhelming because physician owners don't know where to start. When that happens, come back to two anchors: the culture you want to build and the roles and responsibilities you've defined for your staff.

Early onboarding should focus on making sure your team understands how to carry out the vision of the practice, not just what tasks to complete. Your staff need clarity, resources, and context so they can work efficiently and confidently.

When onboarding is rushed or skipped, the downstream effects are real. You'll see inefficiency. Errors happen more easily. Turnover increases. Frustration builds for you and for your team. What feels like saving time upfront often costs far more time and energy later.

When training and onboarding your team, there may be times when you say something one day and come back the next and say, *I thought about this, and I'd like to do it differently.* That's okay. This is your practice. Training is not about rigidity, it's about alignment.

Keep in mind that it's also okay to bring in help. If billing and coding aren't your strengths, bring in someone who can train your front desk staff properly. If workflow needs refinement, you can involve someone with expertise there. Delegating training doesn't mean disengaging. You still need to understand what's happening in your practice, but you should use available resources wisely.

Onboarding and training are where you build the foundation for efficiency. The time you invest here is not wasted. It pays off in smoother days, clearer expectations, and a team that feels equipped rather than overwhelmed.

CHAPTER 28

Shaping the Culture of Your Practice

Some physicians believe that culture is fluff or that it's not something you can intentionally create, but something that just happens on its own.

Often, that belief comes from not seeing enough good examples. Many physicians have never worked in a practice where the flow felt healthy, the environment felt supportive, and the culture felt aligned with good medicine. When you haven't seen it done well, it's easy to assume culture is either irrelevant or out of your control.

But culture is not about personality or popularity. And it's not just about liking the people you work with. In a medical practice, culture is the way people treat each other, patients included. It's the level of respect shown to patients, to leadership, and to the work itself. It's how the day feels when things are busy. It's how the team responds when something goes wrong.

Culture shows up in small, daily moments. It's present in how staff speak to one another. In how they speak to patients. In how problems are addressed instead of ignored. In how stress is managed during a packed clinic day. In how mistakes are handled and whether they're met with blame or with accountability and learning.

All of those moments together create the culture of your practice. And as the physician owner, you set the tone.

One of the most common mistakes I see physicians make is assuming culture will take care of itself. When culture isn't defined intentionally, it gets defined by default, by stress, by habits carried over from previous workplaces, or by the strongest personalities in the room.

A common mistake is expecting behaviors from staff that you don't model yourself. Culture isn't built through policies alone. It's built through what you tolerate, what you reinforce, and how you show up daily. If respect, communication, and professionalism matter to you, those values have to be visible in your leadership.

When culture isn't shaped intentionally, the downstream effects are real. Burnout becomes more common, turnover increases, tension builds between staff members, inefficiencies multiply, and over time, the practice begins to feel heavier than it needs to be.

Culture doesn't require perfection. It requires clarity and consistency. When you're intentional about the environment you're building, you create a practice that supports both your patients and your team.

CHAPTER 29

Learning to Delegate Without Losing Control

Somewhere during medical training, many physicians absorb a false narrative: *If you want something done right, you have to do it yourself.* That belief may help you survive training, but it does not serve you in private practice.

In fact, believing you're the only one who can do certain tasks is one of the fastest ways to recreate the very burnout you were likely trying to escape. Most physicians don't pursue private practice to work themselves into a different version of exhaustion. They do it to build something more sustainable.

And yet, delegation is still hard.

Most physicians struggle with delegation because they believe it's faster to do things themselves. They worry others will make mistakes. They believe they can do things the "right" way more efficiently. And many physicians carry a deep sense of responsibility tied to their identity, the practice of being the one who is accountable for everything in front of them.

That sense of ownership doesn't disappear when you become a practice owner. In some ways, it intensifies. Delegating can feel like losing oversight. It can feel risky. It can feel uncomfortable, especially if you're used to being the person who catches every detail.

But delegation isn't about letting go of responsibility. It's about deciding *where* your responsibility is most needed.

With clear direction, it's not only appropriate but necessary to pass off tasks that don't require your medical training or your direct oversight as owner. There are many things in a practice that must be done, but not necessarily by you.

Some of the most common mistakes I see physicians make when delegating come down to timing and clarity. It is a mistake to delegate without clear expectations. When you assign a task, it's important to be clear about the outcome you want. You don't need to dictate every step, but the person receiving the task should understand what success looks like. Another mistake is waiting too long to delegate. Many physicians wait until they are already overwhelmed and at the brink of burnout before they start handing things off. At that point, delegation feels reactive instead of strategic.

One of the biggest obstacles to effective delegation is micromanaging. Once you've clarified expectations, you have to allow people to do the work. Hovering, redoing tasks, or constantly stepping back in undermines trust and keeps you tethered to the very work you were trying to offload.

Delegation is not about losing control. It's about removing from your plate the tasks that don't require you so that you can focus on the work that only you can do. When done well, delegation frees your time to think, plan, and lead rather than constantly react.

When physicians don't delegate, the consequences add up. Burnout becomes more likely. Bottlenecks form. Growth stalls. And over time, the practice becomes dependent on you for everything, which limits both its potential and your quality of life.

Delegation is not a personality trait. It's not something you're either good at or bad at. Delegation is a skill. And like any other skill in medicine, it can be learned, practiced, and refined over time.

Not finding perfect people or having every answer, but learning how to build a team that allows the practice to function with steadiness and care. The hiring, training, culture, and delegation decisions you've considered here are not about control. They are about creating clarity and shared responsibility.

With the right team in place, the day begins to feel more sustainable, work is clearer, and communication improves. The practice is no longer held together by effort alone, but by systems and relationships that support the work.

Section VII: Leading Through the Early Days

Opening your doors is a big milestone, but it's not the end of the work.

For many physicians, there's a quiet expectation that once the practice is open, things will feel settled. That clarity will arrive. That confidence will be automatic. That the hardest decisions are behind you.

In reality, the early days of private practice are not about arrival, they're about adjustment.

This section is meant to normalize what happens after the launch. The emotions, the learning curve, the moments of doubt, and the steady growth that follows when you stay intentional. These chapters are not about perfection or rapid success. They are about resilience, perspective, and leadership.

Private practice is built over time. And the way you move through these early stages matters just as much as the planning that came before them.

After the Doors Open

Many physicians expect that once the doors open on opening day, everything will feel settled. That the hardest work is behind them. That from that point on, things will start to run smoothly.

I believed that too.

I remember thinking that once the practice was open, the planning and preparation would finally pay off, that things would simply work. I made the decision not to slow-walk into my schedule. We had a good staff, we trained intentionally, and we onboarded thoughtfully. I felt confident that we could move straight into a full clinic.

Those early days hit hard. They tested our systems immediately and exposed where adjustments were needed. It wasn't a failure, it was information. The pace forced us to see what worked in real time and what needed to change.

Emotionally, those first days were complicated. There was confidence and doubt happening at the same time. Relief that the practice had finally opened, paired with the sudden weight of realizing that this was now mine to carry. The responsibility felt real in a way it hadn't before.

Even in the middle of that intensity, though, there was confirmation. Not that everything was perfect, but that I had done what I set out to do. I had built something intentionally. Something with the potential to be sustainable. Something I could work on every day and shape over time.

At the end of that first week, when things finally slowed down, I remember sitting quietly in the clinic. I looked at the flowers that had been sent. I re-read the cards for the third time. And I remember thinking, *Wow. I actually did this. I started a private practice.*

Years later, I still think about those early weeks, but differently. Now, when I look back, I don't just think about the moment of starting. I think about how much the practice has evolved since then, how many changes we've made, and how much better it fits what I wanted it to become.

What I wish I had understood more clearly in those early days is that the intention in starting was never to create something perfect. It was to create something I could build into exactly what I wanted it to be.

And that work didn't end on opening day. It had just begun.

CHAPTER 30

Opening Day Isn't the Finish Line

Most physicians believe that opening day means the hard part is over.

In reality, opening day is just the beginning. Not the beginning of something harder, but the beginning of what you've been working toward all along.

When physicians reach opening day, the emotions are often mixed. There is excitement and fear. Relief and panic. Pride in what has been built, alongside the realization that this thing is now real. Every physician experiences it a little differently, but nearly all share that sense of, *I actually did this.*

What often surprises physician owners most in the first few days or weeks is that things don't go as smoothly as planned. You can plan extensively, and you should, but no amount of planning fully replaces getting into the clinic, seeing patients, and watching how things actually flow. Those early days are when you discover whether the workflows you designed work in real life, not just on paper.

And this is where the beauty of private practice shows up. In private practice, you can adjust. You can say, *We talked about doing it this way, but it's not working, let's change it.* That kind of real-time flexibility is nearly impossible in an employed model, and it's one of the most powerful advantages of ownership.

Opening day and the weeks that follow are also when many physicians realize that the topics covered earlier in this book really do matter. Systems may start to break down if they weren't built intentionally. Staff may have more questions than expected if onboarding wasn't thorough. Workflow issues become obvious when patient volume begins to build. None of this means you did something wrong, It means you're learning what your practice actually needs.

Opening day does not have to define the rest of your career in private practice. If the day feels wonderful, that's great. If it's anything less than wonderful, that's okay too. Both are opportunities to learn. The early days give you valuable information about what's working and what needs to change.

One of the most common mistakes I see physicians make right after opening is judging the future of their practice too quickly. If opening day goes well, some physicians assume success is guaranteed and ease up on marketing, team building, or continued refinement. If opening day is chaotic, others assume failure, that the practice is doomed, and begin making decisions from fear instead of clarity.

Another mistake is comparison. New practices are often measured against long-established ones, without accounting for time, trust, and community presence. Building a practice takes patience as you craft how the practice will live in your own mind and in the minds of patients and referral sources.

The early days will include inefficiencies. There will be uncertainty. You'll learn in real time. And there will be emotional ups and downs. But when you've planned thoughtfully and when you understand that ownership gives you the ability to respond and adapt, those challenges feel manageable instead of overwhelming.

Opening day is not the finish line. It's the starting point for the work of building a practice that grows, evolves, and improves over time.

CHAPTER 31

The First 90 Days

Most physicians expect the first 90 days to prove success or failure.

In reality, much like opening day, the first 90 days are not a verdict. They are a period of discovery. This window is about learning what works, what doesn't, and what needs refinement in the practice you've built. Always remember that you are allowed to change things that aren't working. That flexibility is one of the greatest strengths of private practice.

During the first three months, it's common for practice owners to experience emotional swings. Confidence may rise one week and dip the next. Second-guessing often creeps in, *Was this the right decision? Did I do this too soon?*

This is why your mission statement matters. Your mission statement is what anchors you during moments of doubt. It reminds you why you chose private practice in the first place and why this path aligned with your values, your vision for patient care, and your life. When emotions fluctuate, the mission statement provides clarity.

One of the biggest mistakes physicians make in the first 90 days falls into one of two extremes. Some change too much, too fast. They don't give systems time to settle or allow the team to fully adjust. Everything feels urgent, and constant changes create confusion instead of improvement. Others make the opposite mistake. They see things clearly not working; maybe there are inefficiencies, breakdowns in flow, or communication issues, but they hesitate to step in and adjust. They wait too long, hoping problems will resolve themselves. The balance between these two extremes is delicate, but it's an essential skill of ownership.

The first 90 days are not about perfection. They're about observation and refinement. This is the time to track trends rather than react to single days. One slow clinic or one chaotic afternoon doesn't define your practice. Look for patterns over time and use that information to guide thoughtful adjustments.

This period is also critical for paying attention to your team. Watch how communication is happening. Notice how stress is managed. Be intentional about the culture that's taking shape. Consistency, both individually and as a practice, matters deeply during this phase.

Ultimately, the first 90 days are about refining systems. You are learning what your practice needs to function smoothly in real life, not just in theory. Changes during this time are normal, they are expected, and they are part of building a practice that actually works.

It is normal to make adjustments during the first 90 days. It's actually expected. This phase isn't about proving yourself. It's about leading with clarity, patience, and intention as your practice begins to find its footing.

CHAPTER 32

When Things Feel Hard (and They Will)

Most physicians believe that once the practice is open, they will suddenly feel like a CEO.

In reality, that shift doesn't always happen automatically. Becoming an owner often requires an intentional mindset change, a shift from thinking like an employee to thinking like an employer. And that transition takes time.

Especially early on, building a private practice can feel hard some days.

Whether it's weeks in, months in, or just after the adrenaline of launching wears off, many physicians experience moments where things feel heavier than expected. This doesn't mean something has gone wrong. It usually means you're still in the process of shaping the practice into what you envisioned.

You may have spent months planning, but once the doors open, the work isn't finished. The real-world version of your practice still needs refinement. And that's where the "hard" often shows up.

Hard can take many forms.

It may look like emotional fatigue, carrying the weight of decisions and responsibility day after day. It may show up as financial anxiety, especially when numbers fluctuate or don't yet look the way you hoped. Sometimes it's decision fatigue, the sense that everything requires your input. And sometimes it's simply the feeling of being responsible for more than you've ever been responsible for before.

When these moments happen, many physicians turn inward with harsh conclusions: *Maybe I made a mistake. Maybe I'm not cut out for this. Maybe this was a bad idea.*

When things feel hard, it does not mean you made the wrong decision to start a private practice. More often, it means you need to pause, look objectively at what's in front of you, and decide what adjustments will help move you forward. Hard moments are signals, not verdicts.

Perspective matters here. Stepping back to assess what is working and what isn't can turn emotion into information. Having support, especially from other physicians who own practices, can make these moments feel far less isolating. And revisiting your original motivation matters more than you might expect.

Think back to how you felt when you first decided to pursue private practice. Remember what drew you to this path. Let that clarity guide you when emotions start to cloud your judgment.

And just as importantly, give yourself grace. You gave yourself grace during medical school. You gave yourself grace during training. You are allowed to extend that same compassion to yourself now. Building a private practice is a skill and, like any skill, it develops over time.

Feeling challenged does not mean you are failing. Feeling stretched does not mean you are on the wrong path. Often, it simply means you are growing into a role you were meant to hold.

CHAPTER 33

Growing With Intention

Most physicians think growth means seeing more patients or adding more services.

And while those things can certainly be part of building a successful practice, growth without intention can quickly turn into something that feels familiar, in the worst way.

Unintentional growth often looks like being busy but increasingly chaotic. It shows up when you start adding services because you feel pressure to do so, not because those services align with what you actually want to offer. It can feel like losing control of your schedule, or watching the culture you worked hard to create slowly erode as things move faster than you expected.

In other words, the practice is growing but you're not necessarily happier.

Intentional growth looks different. It's measured and thoughtful. It's not reactive. It gives you space to pause and ask, *Does this next step actually support the practice I set out to build?*

When growth is intentional, decisions are made with clarity rather than urgency. You're not expanding because you feel like you have to. You're expanding because it makes sense for your patients, your team, and your life.

One of the most common mistakes I see physicians make once things start going well is expanding too quickly. Early success creates momentum, and momentum can feel exciting. But when expansion outpaces systems, staffing, or personal capacity, the practice begins to drift. The mission that anchored the practice at the beginning starts to fade into the background. And without realizing it, physicians can recreate the very burnout they were trying to escape when they chose private practice.

Growth should never come at the expense of sustainability. When you're deciding whether to grow, there are a few anchors worth returning to again and again.

Start with your mission. Why did you build this practice in the first place? Does this next step support that vision or pull you away from it?

Look at the numbers. What did you forecast for growth when you planned this practice? Are you ahead, behind, or right on track? Growth that isn't supported by the math eventually creates strain.

Consider your capacity and your season of life. Growth that makes sense at one stage may not make sense at another. There is no single "right" pace, only the pace that works for you.

You are allowed to say no to opportunities that don't align. You are allowed to move slower than others expect. And you are allowed to prioritize stability, clarity, and joy over constant expansion.

Choose growth on your terms. Growth that strengthens your practice rather than stretches it thin. Growth that honors the reason you started this journey in the first place.

Intentional growth is not about doing more. It's about building a practice that continues to work for you.

This section was about steadiness.

Not avoiding difficulty or forcing growth, but learning how to lead when the practice is new, the emotions are real, and the outcomes are still unfolding. The early days are not a test of whether you made the right decision. They are a period of adjustment, learning, and leadership.

With time, patterns emerge. Confidence grows quietly. The work becomes less reactive and more intentional. What once felt heavy begins to feel familiar. You are not behind. You are becoming the kind of leader this phase requires.

Conclusion: Choosing Private Practice, On Purpose

If you've made it this far, pause for a moment.

Not because you've reached the end of the book, but because you've walked through a way of thinking that most physicians are never invited into.

You didn't just read about private practice. You considered whether ownership could actually work *for you*.

For most physicians, private practice begins as a quiet question. One that shows up after a hard clinic day, after another decision is made without your input, or after realizing that the way medicine is being practiced around you no longer feels sustainable or aligned. That question is rarely loud. And it's rarely impulsive.

It sounds more like:

Could this really be different?

Is there another way to practice medicine?

Do I have what it takes to build something of my own?

Throughout this book, we've slowed those questions down.

You've explored mindset shifts that challenge the stories many of us were taught about risk, profitability, and responsibility. You've thought intentionally about mission, practice design, finances, infrastructure, marketing, team-building, and growth. Not as abstract concepts but as real decisions that shape daily life.

And perhaps most importantly, you've seen that private practice is not about doing everything perfectly or knowing everything upfront. It's about intention.

Private practice, when done well, is not accidental. It is designed by physicians who are willing to think differently, ask better questions, and build systems that support both patient care *and* physician well-being.

If there's one truth I hope you carry with you, it's this: Feeling uncertain does not mean you are unqualified. Feeling stretched does not mean you made the wrong decision. Feeling challenged does not mean you should turn back. It means you are learning something new.

You already know how to do hard things. You proved that when you went to medical school, you proved it during training, and you prove it every day you show up for patients. Building a private practice is not harder than what you've already done, it's just different.

And you don't have to do it alone.

One of the most damaging myths in medicine is that independence means isolation. That asking for help somehow undermines competence. That ownership requires you to carry every decision, every fear, and every unknown by yourself.

That simply isn't true. Private practice works best when physicians are supported. When they have space to think clearly, run the numbers honestly, make decisions intentionally, and course-correct without panic.

That's exactly why I do this work.

Over the years, I've worked with physicians at every stage of this journey, those who are just beginning to wonder if private practice is possible, and those who are already in motion but want clarity and confidence as they build. The questions are rarely about capability. They're about direction.

So as you close this book, here's my invitation to you: *Choose your next step intentionally.*

If you want help organizing your thoughts and understanding what launching a private practice actually involves, there's a Private Practice Startup Checklist waiting for you.

If you're ready to move from thinking to planning, there's guidance to help you build a clear and usable business plan, one that fits your goals and your life.

And if you want personalized support as you design and launch your practice, there's a way for us to work together one-on-one, physician to physician.

You can access all of these next steps by visiting ***www.hangingashingle.com***.

Whether you choose to work with me or take the next steps on your own, I want you to know something:

Private practice is not reserved for a select few. It is not reckless. And it is not outdated.

It is a viable, meaningful path for physicians who want autonomy, alignment, and a renewed relationship with the work they trained so hard to do.

You are allowed to want that. You are allowed to build it thoughtfully. And you are allowed to choose private practice, on purpose.

About the Author

Dr. Brittney Anderson is a board-certified family medicine physician and private practice owner who believes physicians deserve practices that work for them and for their patients.

After working in employed models, Dr. Anderson made the decision to step away and build her own independent practice. What began as a desire for greater autonomy became a deeper commitment to practicing medicine with intention, sustainability, and clarity. Today, she owns and operates a successful private practice while remaining actively engaged in physician leadership, mentorship, and advocacy at the state and national level.

Through her work, Dr. Anderson has helped physicians across the country think realistically and practically about private practice, cutting through fear-based narratives and oversimplified advice to focus on what actually matters. She is the creator of *The Private Practice Blueprint Coaching* and the *Plan to Practice Digital Course*, and she works with physicians one-on-one to help them design practices that align with their values, goals, and season of life.

She also hosts the podcast *Physicians Hanging a Shingle*, where she explores the mindset, strategy, and real-world decisions behind private practice ownership. The show features candid conversations and practical guidance for physicians who are considering, or actively building, their own practices.

Dr. Anderson is known for her grounded, honest approach to ownership. She does not believe private practice is the right path for everyone, but she does believe every physician deserves the clarity to decide intentionally. Her work centers on helping physicians slow down, ask better questions, and build practices on purpose rather than by default.

She lives and practices in Alabama and continues to care for patients while supporting physicians who are ready to imagine, and build, something different.